Hope

FOUR WEEK MINI BIBLE STUDY

Heather Bixler

Becoming Press, LLC

Heather Bixler/Becoming Press, LLC
www.becomingpress.com

Ordering Information:
Quantity sales. Special discounts are available on quantity purchases by corporations, associations, and others. For details, contact the "Special Sales Department" at the address above.

Hope - Four Week Mini Bible Study/ Heather Bixler—1st ed.
ISBN-13: 978-1978475472
ISBN-10: 1978475470

Scripture quotations are from The World English Bible.

Table of Contents

Introduction

One morning I was talking with my husband and I felt I needed to tell him what was on my heart about his chronic illness. I told him that ever since he got sick my security in the quote "everything will be OK" was gone. Before he got sick, I knew that tomorrow was never guaranteed, nor was a good, healthy life, either. But now, I finally felt insecurity, even though his disease isn't necessarily life threatening. However, since he had gotten sick, our life had changed dramatically and his disease affects him every time he eats, so it is something we are reminded of often.

After I confided in him what he said struck me; he said, "No matter what happens, God will always be there." In that moment I realized that I was seeking security and hope in all the wrong things. In fact my ONLY security and hope can be found in the presence of God! Then and there I began my journey to find satisfaction with His presence only, through everything, good and bad, desperate and content, lustful or satisfied, insecure or at peace. His presence needs to be enough no matter what we are going through.

I hope you will take this journey with me through the pages of this book, and I pray this book is a blessing to you!

About Achalasia

In this Bible Study I talk a lot about my husband's disease. When I refer to his disease I am talking about achalasia. Achalasia is a rare disease that affects the esophagus and lower esophageal sphincter. There is no cure, and typically the symptoms can be manage with a surgery called a Heller Myotomy.

About Faith, Hope, and Love

But now faith, hope, and love remain--these three. The greatest of these is love.
- 1 Corinthians 13:13

This book is the first book in a four week mini Bible Study series I did on 1 Corinthians 13:13. Over the past three years God has taken me on a journey to shift my perspective to eternity. We can get so bogged down with the circumstances we face in life.

Every day that I wake up I can't help but think why I was so fortunate to wake up and be alive TODAY!

When our heart is set on eternity then we learn to live for today and we are never hesitant to be all that God created us to be.

Why faith, hope, and love? Because these three things will go on forever - this is what we need to focus on, today.

Everything else will crumble, but your faith, hope, and love will go on for all eternity. That is the message you will find in this four week mini-Bible study series. You can learn more about the Bible Studies and the author at: www.BecomingPress.com.

Hope Foundation

"Not only this, but we also rejoice in our sufferings, knowing that suffering works perseverance; and perseverance, proven character; and proven character, hope: and hope doesn't disappoint us, because God's love has been poured out into our hearts through the Holy Spirit who was given to us." - **Romans 5:3-5**

It took me awhile to get to the point where I stopped praying for God to give me what I wanted, and instead pray for what **He** wanted.

Waiting for my husband to be healed from his disease was depressing. But in my mind I was clinging to hope that God can, and would, heal my husband.

It took me awhile to realize that faith and hope isn't about what you will receive, it is about what you believe.

It takes great faith to trust that no matter what happens, God is still good. When we have that kind of faith then we have hope in the presence of the Spirit in our life.

Maybe as a society we have "hope" all wrong. We hope for provision, success, healing, a bigger house, children, and relationships. Our view on hope needs to be changed. We need the light of the truth to be shined on what hope really is.

In Romans 5:3-5 it shows us that hope comes through trials. Suffering, perseverance, character, then comes hope. Hope isn't a wish or a dream – hope is a way of thinking and it's a way of living. Hope is born from the strength and confidence that only comes from the Spirit. That's where hope lives and gives us the motivation to keep pressing forward with a joyful heart.

Hope isn't about waiting for our desires to be fulfilled. Hope is knowing the Holy Spirit and leaning into His presence that is always with us. This is hope...it is knowing that no matter what, God is good and He is always with you.

Life Application

"It took me awhile to realize that faith and hope isn't about what you will receive, it is about what you believe.."

- Do you think of hope as wanting and waiting for your desires to be manifested in your life?
- What if your desires are not in line with God's will for your life? What if they are?
- Will wishful thinking make God's will happen faster in your life?
- Will anything that is in line with God's sovereign will happen before, or after, He chooses it to happen?
- Can you put your hope in His sovereign will?
- Will you trust in Him and find hope in His presence through anything that may happen in your life?

Week One Scripture Journal

Week One Memory Verse:
Proverbs 24:14.

Day One: Write down the scripture you are learning in the space provided below:

Day Two: Write scripture down four times on a sticky note and place them around the house.

Day Three: Look up 3 different versions of the scripture. Write them in the space provided below:

Day Four: Write scripture 10x's in the space provided below:

Day Five: Read Proverbs 24 and journal your thoughts in the space provided below:

Day Six: Write scripture by memory 3x's in the space provided below:

Day Seven: Share your scripture with a friend.

Discussion Questions

The following questions are designed to be used within a group discussion about the scripture you memorized.

- How do you define wisdom? How do you define understanding? Look up these words in the dictionary and discuss the definition.
- Name three foolish behaviors outlined in Proverbs 24. Do you see any of these being displayed in your own life.
- How can these behaviors prevent you from having a mind that is focused on the Spirit? How do they steal your hope?

WEEK TWO

Hope Crisis

If we have only hoped in Christ in this life, we are of all men most pitiable. - **1 Corinthians 15:19**

When someone you love passes away or gets sick, you most certainly go through a hope crisis. Everything you had been hoping for gets shaken and broken down so that you may even begin to lose hope all together. You may even begin to have thoughts that this life is just random, or you are out of God's will, or maybe you have done something wrong. You may find that your hope was centered on your loved one getting better, then after the disappointment of seeing them continue with their illness, or even pass away, hope may slowly begin to fade away too.

After my husband was diagnosed with his disease I actually found my hope again, because for several years we had no idea what was wrong with my husband. It was nice to finally have some answers and a plan in place that would hopefully make him better. After we found out that the surgery didn't work, that was when I had my hope crisis. In that moment all security in the plans we had for the future were gone. No one could tell me that everything was going to be OK. The surgery was supposed to make everything OK. My hope was wrapped up in this surgery. As soon as my husband started having symptoms again I could feel the fear creep in again. It was gut-wrenching. Truthfully, it still is.

When we find ourselves in a hope crisis we are at a place where we need to rebuild. We need to figure out Who God is and what role He plays in our life. A hope crisis can tear down our relationship with Him only so we can rebuild a stronger, more sturdy, relationship with God. Sometimes we may choose not to rebuild, but where is the hope in that?

Its like a marriage that is built on lies. Once the lies are discovered, everything that had been built on those lies comes crumbling down. The couple needs to re-build, but this time the marriage will be stronger and better, if they choose to take the time and effort to make things right.

If our hope in God and the future is based on a hope that is designed to give and never take, then our hope will come crumbling down when we face a hope crisis. Often our hope is based on what we will receive in this life rather than what we believe to be true about God. But within our hope crisis, our shaky, selfish hope comes tumbling down. But if we turn to God in this moment and do the work, then we will rebuild a hope in our heart that cannot be shaken by even the hardest tragedies and trials. Then we can build our hope on God's sovereignty rather than on what He can do for us.

Life Application

"Often our hope is based on what we will receive in this life rather than what we believe to be true about God."

- Have you ever had a hope crisis?
- When you lost hope in the Lord was it based on what He could do for you in this world?
- Look at 1 Corinthians 15:19 – what does this scripture mean to you?

Through Jesus we have hope in the eternal life, not just here in the world. When we have a hope crisis our hope is weak and it reveals the lack of hope we have towards the eternal future.

- Why is it pitiful for us to only have hope in Christ for what He can do for us in this world rather than what He has already done for us in the eternal?
- What do you think about the statement?:

Week Two Scripture Journal

Week Two Memory Verse:
1 Peter 1: 3,4.

Day One: Write down the scripture you are learning in the space provided below:

Day Two: Write scripture down four times on a sticky note and place them around the house.

Day Three: Look up 3 different versions of the scripture. Write them in the space provided below:

Day Four: Write scripture 10x's in the space provided below:

Day Five: Read 1 Peter Chapter one and journal your thoughts in the space provided below:

Day Six: Write scripture by memory 3x's in the space provided below:

Day Seven: Share your scripture with a friend.

Discussion Questions

The following questions are designed to be used within a group discussion about the scripture you memorized.

- According to 1 Peter chapter 1, where will we find our inheritance?
- How can our trials bring God praise and glory?
- Where are we to set our hope?

Get Up

For we were saved in hope, but hope that is seen is not hope. For who hopes for that which he sees? 25But if we hope for that which we don't see, we wait for it with patience. - **Romans 8:24-25**

As I listened to the sermon at church on Sunday I could clearly hear the Lord say to me "Get up! Stop feeling sorry for yourself. I have a plan for you!"

The truth is I had been playing the victim in my sufferings. The pity party prevailed. I was just getting by through the days and it was showing in my house, my writing, and my kiddos' behavior. Sleeping all day sounded GOOD.

But although I lay victim to my circumstances, God never lost hope in me. Even though the enemy questioned my obedience to God in all circumstances, God never questioned it. His purpose set before me, as painful as it may be, reveals that He still believes in me.

Sometimes our heart focuses on removing the suffering, or we are expecting a miracle. But sometimes the miracle is finding hope in all circumstances.

So many beautiful things can happen in one day; many tragic things can happen in the same day. It has been made apparently clear in the Bible that our faith in Jesus does not remove suffering from our life. Every day we must suffer through the death of our flesh in order to meet with the Holy Spirit.

The only real guarantee we have in this Christian life is that we are not victims of our circumstances. No matter what, we can still hope, have faith, and show love to one another. We can still be obedient to God and His plan for our life.

In the midst of our tragedies and greatest heartaches we can either choose to be a victim or we can chose obedience to God. What was Satan implying when he wanted to test Job and said, *"Does Job fear God for nothing?"* (Job 1:9) He was asking God if Job would *STILL* obey God in all circumstances.

When all hope seems lost we have a choice: Are we going to rebel or are we going to remain obedient to God?

Life Application

"But although I lay victim to my circumstances, God never lost hope in me."

- How can our patience stop us from hoping?
- When you lose hope do you also lose motivation to do the daily tasks? Why is your hope lost?
- Is it because God has not met your expectation? Has he not answered a prayer?
- List three prayers He HAS answered recently?
- What role do these answered prayers play in the unanswered prayers?
- Are you willing to obey God in all circumstances even if your prayers are not answered?

Week Three Scripture Journal

Week Two Memory Verse:
Romans 12:12.

Day One: Write down the scripture you are learning in the space provided below:.

Day Two: Write scripture down four times on a sticky note and place them around the house.

Day Three: Look up 3 different versions of the scripture. Write them in the space provided below:

Day Four: Write scripture 10x's in the space provided below:

Day Five: Read Romans Chapter 12 and journal your thoughts in the space provided below:

Day Six: Write scripture by memory 3x's in the space provided below:

Day Seven: Share your scripture with a friend.

Discussion Questions

The following questions are designed to be used within a group discussion about the scripture you memorized.

- How can we present our bodies as "Living sacrifice, holy and acceptable to God?"
- How has God designed the body of Christ? With this amazing design how is God's sovereignty amplified?
- How can slothfulness prevent us from being a true servant of Christ?

WEEK FOUR

My Insecurity

For whatever things were written before were written for our learning, that through patience and through encouragement of the Scriptures we might have hope.
- Romans 15:4

The more I walk down this road the more insecure I feel. Every step I can feel the Lord stripping away every little thing I hide behind, everything I define myself with and find my security in.

From my husband's health, to placing me in situations that aren't all that comfortable for me, to the instability within my husband's job right now, and the constant change and shifts that are happening in my life right now; I often look for stability and security in new and different things.

When we feel insecure and vulnerable in life, it can be quite easy to turn to sin. Or maybe you grit your teeth and look for people and things to control. I think the enemy likes to use insecurity to scare us back into a life of false control and the illusion of comfort. Sadly, we stay in this place and hide ourselves in isolation when in fact His grace, peace, and hope are found in those moments of insecurity and vulnerability.

I found through my desire to find security once again, I began to leave the power of The Holy Spirit behind in hopes that I would somehow find a way to be safe. If we are going to find hope in the midst of every circumstance we need to be willing to let go of the desire to be safe and embrace the desire to simply be in His presence.

When it seems all hope is lost we can easily find it again by looking towards the vision that God has placed in our heart for that day, and quickly responding to the small intuitive nudging of the Holy Spirit. Do we know what tomorrow will bring? Are we able to decipher the BIG plan God has for our life? I don't think we can, and yet we try to every single day when really our only need and worry is to figure out what it is God has for us TODAY.

Letting go of control and surrendering the dark foggy future is truly the only way to find hope again. That was my goal for this book, to somehow find hope among all that is swirling around me, and I did. I hope you did too.

Life Application

"If we are going to find hope in the midst of every circumstance we need to be willing to let go of the desire to be safe and embrace the desire to simply be in His presence."

- How can letting go of the future help us find hope for today?
- What is the Holy Spirit nudging you to do right now? If you cannot here the Holy Spirit, take a minute to write out a prayer asking the Holy Spirit to speak to you. Be willing to surrender your thoughts and ideas to the Holy Spirit. Allow the Holy Spirit to guide your the thoughts that enter your heart and mind.
- What steps can you take today to live a life that is less safe and filled with more insecurity and vulnerability? Once you take those steps journal the results and what miracles you experienced.

Week Four Scripture Journal

Week Two Memory Verse:
Romans 15:13.

Day One: Write down the scripture you are learning in the space provided below:

Day Two: Write scripture down four times on a sticky note and place them around the house.

Day Three: Look up 3 different versions of the scripture. Write them in the space provided below:

Day Four: Write scripture 10x's in the space provided below:

Day Five: Read Romans chapter 15 and journal your thoughts in the space provided below:

Day Six: Write scripture by memory 3x's in the space provided below:

Day Seven: Share your scripture with a friend.

Discussion Questions

The following questions are designed to be used within a group discussion about the scripture you memorized.

- How can acts of service put us in a place of vulnerability and insecurity?
- How can serving others help us to find our hope again?
- Have you ever experienced a miracle while serving another person? If so journal or share what that miracle was with the group.

Conclusion

As I finish up this eBook I am preparing for Christmas (it's is now Christmas Eve) and my heart feels heavy. I think about my own little desires. The desire that my husband would be completely healed from his disease, and how he is still suffering through this every day. It is all hurting my heart, and then I think about hope.

How do we find hope in the daily living with the desires in our heart that have yet to be fulfilled? Honestly, I find it very fitting to be ending this Bible Study on hope during Christmas. Who can bring us the hope we so desires? It's Jesus.

So many things can't be fully explained or even made better. Sometimes our circumstances leave us at a point where we simply need to endure through some of the most painful times in our life. Even in that, as we learn to completely rely on and trust in the sovereignty of God, we learn to trust and HOPE that all things can and will work together for the greater good.

The suffering of Jesus, the sacrifice of God, the power of the Holy Spirit; this is where we find our hope. This is where we find the strength to continue to walk this long, lonely road that is filled with many heart breaks and even more pain. Often when the suffering isn't removed, or we are asked by God to endure, we lose our faith in Him, and then in turn lose our hope. When tragedy strikes and we are left to endure the pain, the last thing we need to do is turn our back on the One that is our ONLY hope.

I hope you will be encouraged to never give up on God, and realize that hope is not found in the removal of our suffering, but instead it is found in the faith we have in God, His Son, and the Holy Spirit.

About the Author

Heather is a mom of three, married to a firefighter, and she is a writer. She is passionate about sharing God's word in a practical and loving way.

He has said to me, "My grace is sufficient for you, for my power is made perfect in weakness." Most gladly therefore I will rather glory in my weaknesses, that the power of Christ may rest on me.- **2 Cor 12:9**

Follow Heather

- **Author Blog:** HeatherBixler.com
- **Twitter:** @hbixler03
- **Facebook:** HeatherBixlerWrites
- **Pinterest:** @hbixler03
- **Instagram:** @hbixler03
- **Etsy:** http://ilovewordsart.com

Audiobooks

If you like audiobooks then be sure to check out Heather's audiobooks on audible and iTunes!

Reviews Needed!

I would love to hear your feedback - please leave your reviews of Hope - Four Week Mini Bible Study online wherever books are sold!

More Resources

To view more practical Bible Studies visit:

http://becomingpress.com

More Books by Heather

Be You – Four Week Mini Bible Study

Breaking Pride: Tearing Down Walls, Walking in His Grace

Desires of My Heart: Meditation on Psalm 37:4

Devotions for Moms: Thirty-Seven Devotionals

Faith – Four Week Mini Bible Study

Hope – Four Week Mini Bible Study

Love - Four Week Mini Bible Study

My Scripture Journal: Fearing the Lord

My Scripture Journal: Gratitude

My Scripture Journal: The Promises of God

My Treasures - Four Week Mini Bible Study

Rejected - Four Week Mini Bible Study

Worship is This - Four Week Mini Bible Study

Made in the USA
Middletown, DE
11 August 2023